The Science of A Volcanic Eruption

Samantha Bell

Published in the United States of America by Cherry Lake Publishing
Ann Arbor, Michigan
www.cherrylakepublishing.com

Consultants: Jennifer Rivers Cole, Department of Earth and Planetary Sciences, Harvard University;
Marla Conn, ReadAbility, Inc.
Editorial direction: Red Line Editorial
Book design and illustration: Design Lab

Photo Credits: Pablo Hidalgo/Shutterstock Images, cover, 1; Herbert M. Herget/National Geographic Society/Corbis, 5;
Stefano Bianchetti/Corbis, 6; Nick Hall/Thinkstock, 9; James Stevenson/Donks Models/DK Images, 10; AP Images, 15;
Twonix Studio/Shutterstock Images, 17; Design Lab, 19; Dr. Morley Read/Shutterstock Images, 23; Bettmann/Corbis, 24;
Maridav/Shutterstock Images, 28

Library of Congress Cataloging-in-Publication Data
Bell, Samantha, author.
  The science of a volcanic eruption / by Samantha Bell.
    pages cm. -- (Disaster science)
  Audience: Age 11.
  Audience: Grades 4 to 6.
  Includes bibliographical references and index.
  ISBN 978-1-63137-628-3 (hardcover) -- ISBN 978-1-63137-673-3 (pbk.) -- ISBN 978-1-63137-718-1 (pdf ebook) --
ISBN 978-1-63137-763-1 (hosted ebook)
  1. Volcanism--Juvenile literature. 2. Volcanoes--Juvenile literature. 3. Volcanic activity prediction--Juvenile literature.
I. Title.

  QE522.B39 2015
  551.21--dc23   2014004034

Cherry Lake Publishing would like to acknowledge the work of
The Partnership for 21st Century Skills. Please visit www.p21.org
for more information.

Printed in the United States of America
Corporate Graphics Inc.
July 2014

ABOUT THE AUTHOR

Samantha Bell has written or illustrated more than 20 books for children. Her interests are as
varied as her books, and she is especially fascinated by the natural world.

TABLE OF CONTENTS

CHAPTER 1

A City Is Destroyed

August 20 of the year 79 CE began as a typical day in the ancient Roman city of Pompeii. People bustled about the marketplace, buying and selling goods such as wine, olives, wool, and onions. Some relaxed in public baths, and others exercised in the gymnasium. Vesuvius, a peak about ten miles (16 km) away, overlooked the city of 15,000 people. For Pompeii, the morning was business as usual. Then the ground began to shake. But the trembling did not worry the people of Pompeii. They did not realize these earthquakes were signs of something much worse to come.

In the afternoon of August 24, smoke billowed up from Vesuvius. The strange sight made some curious. Others became worried. Suddenly, the mountain exploded with massive force. **Magma** and hot gases had been building up pressure within the mountain, and

Pompeii was a peaceful, thriving town before Vesuvius erupted.

People tried to escape Pompeii when it became obvious the city was doomed.

the peak finally gave way. A column of volcanic ash reached many miles high and turned the sky black.

That night around midnight, the first **pyroclastic flow** surged down the side of the mountain facing away from Pompeii. Moving at about 62 miles per hour (100 kmh), it covered the seaside resort town of Herculaneum. Two more waves followed. The fourth rushed down the mountain toward Pompeii. At nearly 575 degrees Fahrenheit (300°C), the heat of the flow instantly killed everything still alive in the city.

THE PEOPLE OF POMPEII

Buried quickly under ash and rock, Pompeii was well preserved. It was rediscovered in the eighteenth century. The victims had long since decomposed, but their bodies left behind empty spaces in the hardened ash. By pouring plaster into these spaces, archaeologists have been able to create casts of the victims in their last moments.

The destruction of Pompeii is a chilling reminder of the deadly power of volcanoes. These powerful forces of nature can erupt with little or no warning. Due to the events of 79 CE, Vesuvius is among the best known volcanoes in history.

Volcanologists now know that earthquakes occurring near a known volcano can signal the volcano will soon erupt. Today, the modern city of Naples sits near Vesuvius. Scientists watch the volcano carefully. It has erupted several times since Pompeii's destruction, and some believe another massive eruption could come soon. This time, scientists want to be ready.

CHAPTER 2

The Making of a Volcano

Volcanoes are among the most destructive natural forces in the solar system. They are found not only on Earth, but also on other planets and their moons. On Earth, explosive eruptions have killed more than 200,000 people in the last 500 years. Scientists have counted a total of about 1,300 volcanoes on the planet. Most have erupted many times throughout history. Today, about 550 volcanoes are still active.

The lithosphere is the surface layer of Earth. It contains the **crust** and the upper part of the **mantle**. Earth's lithosphere is broken up into parts called tectonic plates. The plates slide around very slowly on the mantle's magma. Most of the world's volcanoes are located where tectonic plates meet and magma breaks through to the surface. Some are on land, and others are deep under the sea. Approximately 90 percent of the world's volcanoes are located in the Ring of Fire along the edge of the Pacific Ocean.

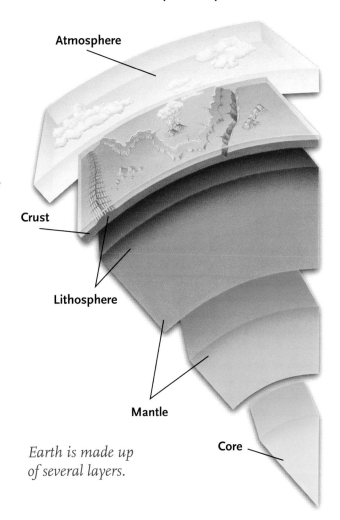

Atmosphere

Crust

Lithosphere

Mantle

Core

Earth is made up of several layers.

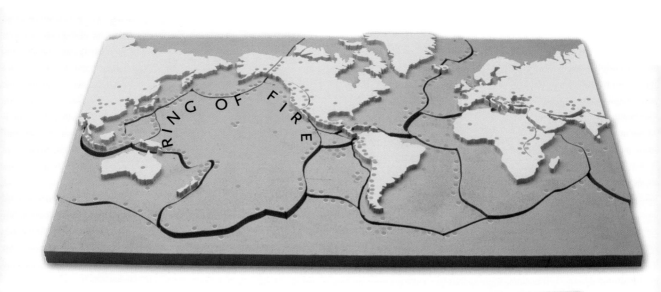

RING OF FIRE

WHERE IN THE WORLD ARE VOLCANOES?

Volcanoes are not scattered randomly across the world. The map above shows Earth's tectonic plates. Volcanoes are shown as red dots. Do you notice a pattern between where plates connect and volcanoes form?

A Volcano Is Born

In 1943, a farmer was working in his fields in Mexico when suddenly the ground began to rise. It exploded with ash, vapors, and lava, creating a cone. By the next day, the cone was already about 164 feet (50 m) high. Today the volcano, known as Paricutín, stands 1,350 feet (410 m) high. It has given scientists a unique opportunity to study a volcano from its formation.

When two tectonic plates meet, they can pull apart, come together, or pass by each other. Volcanoes rarely form when plates simply pass by each other. But if plates pull apart, they create a **rift** between them. The rift fills with hot magma rising up from the upper mantle. The magma cools quickly, forming a new ridge. Volcanoes formed this way are called rift volcanoes, and they rarely rise above sea level. The East African Rift System contains many rift volcanoes.

If tectonic plates meet, the edge of one plate is pushed under the other one. At these areas, called

subduction zones, the plate heats up as it gets pushed downward. The heat pushes magma up toward the surface. On the way to the surface, the magma melts minerals rich with a chemical compound called silica. The silica makes the magma thick and sticky. When the magma erupts through the surface, it is too thick to flow very far. It sticks to the sides of the volcano. Over time this forms a tall, steep cone shape. Mount Rainier and Mount Saint Helens in Washington State are two well-known subduction volcanoes.

Nearly all volcanoes form between tectonic plates, but rarely volcanoes can form in the center of a tectonic plate. Heat can rise from deep inside Earth and melt the rock in the crust. In these hot spots, newly formed magma rises up through cracks in the plate and erupts, forming volcanoes. As the plate slowly moves, the volcano moves along with it, leaving behind islands. The result is a chain of volcanoes, such as the Hawaiian Islands.

New Evidence for an Old Theory

Most scientists accept the theory of moving tectonic plates under Earth's surface. In science, a theory is much more than just a guess. Very strong evidence is needed to call something a theory. By studying volcanoes with modern instruments, scientists have found evidence to support the theory of plate tectonics.

The original ideas about plate tectonics were based on the edges of the continents. On a globe, the continents look as though they could be separated pieces of a puzzle. Newer evidence backs up the theory. Scientists have observed that volcanoes and earthquakes happen mainly at the boundaries of the plates. This is where one would expect to find these things if the theory is true.

CHAPTER 3

TYPES OF VOLCANOES AND ERUPTIONS

Some volcanoes have such small eruptions that tourists can watch them from just a few feet away. Others are so violent they destroy entire cities. Yet all volcanoes have some things in common.

Beneath Earth's crust is the mantle, filled with molten rock and gas. Magma from below flows and collects here until the heat and pressure become too great. The **magma chamber** cannot contain it any longer. The magma rushes up a central vent to Earth's surface. It oozes, gushes, or explodes out of the **summit crater**.

The simplest type of volcano is the cinder cone volcano. Ash explodes from a single vent at the top and falls around the vent in particles and clumps called cinders. The cinders harden, giving the volcano a cone shape. These volcanoes have steep sides. Paricutín in Mexico is an example of a cinder cone volcano.

People rushed to the scene with cameras after Paricutín erupted in 1943.

A shield volcano is formed almost entirely by flowing lava. Lava emerges from the summit vent or a group of vents. It continues to pour out for a long period of time, flowing down the side of the volcano in all directions. This creates a tall, broad, sloping cone. The final shape looks a bit like a warrior's shield lying flat on the ground. The Hawaiian Islands are a chain of shield volcanoes.

The deadliest volcanoes are stratovolcanoes. They are made of alternating layers of volcanic ash, lava flows, and cinders. The layers build up to create a tall, steep

A 30-YEAR ERUPTION

The name of the Hawaiian volcano Kilauea comes from a Hawaiian word meaning "much spreading." The volcano lives up to its name. Since 1983, Kilauea has been erupting slowly and steadily. Over time, it has destroyed small towns and added nearly 1 square mile (2.6 sq km) of land to the island.

volcano. Vesuvius in Italy, Mount Fuji in Japan, and Mount Saint Helens are all stratovolcanoes.

It is important to know which kind of eruption a particular volcano will produce. This way, scientists can help keep people safe if it occurs. Some types of eruptions may have more widespread impacts, requiring a larger

Mount Fuji is the highest and most famous mountain in Japan.

evacuation. Different kinds of eruptions are grouped into categories based on their characteristics. But all eruptions can be classified as either effusive or explosive.

In effusive eruptions, lava rises to the surface in flows or fountains. It can also seep through cracks and form huge pools. When the lava cools, it hardens and fills in the cracks. The slow speed of effusive eruptions allows people to escape their paths. As a result, they rarely kill people.

Explosive eruptions, however, produce many hazards because of their suddenness and speed. They can cause destruction and death on a massive scale. Poisonous gases, rock fragments, and volcanic ash can kill people and animals. Landslides, **lahars**, and pyroclastic flows wipe out everything in their paths. If people do survive, they are often forced to leave their ruined land, homes, and cities.

Volcano Variety

Below are images of each of the three volcano types discussed in this chapter. What key differences do you notice? How might these differences give each type of volcano its shape and structure?

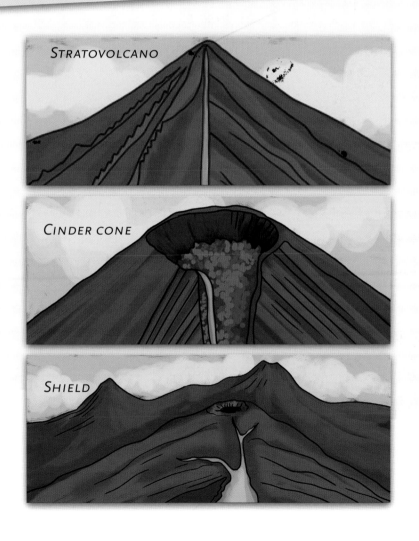

STRATOVOLCANO

CINDER CONE

SHIELD

Violent Volcanoes

Volcanic eruptions can cause dramatic changes to Earth's landscape and climate. Even in places far from the eruption, volcanoes can affect crops, transportation, power supplies, and other parts of everyday life.

Volcanic ash is one of the furthest-reaching volcanic hazards. During a violent eruption, escaping gas rips through solid rock and magma, blasting them into the air. As these materials cool they form ash. Winds can carry the ash hundreds or even thousands of miles away. It can make the sky so dark people can hardly see where they are going. Heavy ashfall can cause roofs to collapse. Rain turns ash-covered roads and highways into slippery mud. Ash clogs and damages cars, jet engines, and water systems.

As ash fills the sky, lava flows ooze or pour from the vent. The flows move down the sides of the volcano, covering and igniting everything in their way. The speed of a flow depends on the type of lava, the steepness of the ground, and how quickly the lava is

ASH AND AIRPLANES

In April 2010, the Eyjafjallajökull volcano in Iceland erupted. The eruption sent a massive cloud of ash into the air. The wind carried it toward Europe. People soon realized that the ash could possibly jam up jet engines, causing passenger planes to crash. Authorities shut down air travel in northern Europe for more than a week, canceling several thousand flights.

coming out of the vent. Some lava flows move as a wide mass, while others travel through a narrow channel. Because the flows move so slowly, people usually have time to get out of the way unharmed if there is some warning. But the land the flow covers becomes hardened rock. Homes, buildings, and farmland are destroyed.

During eruptions, gases in the magma are released into the atmosphere. These gases rise, and the wind spreads them hundreds of miles. Many different gases are produced, including sulfur dioxide, carbon dioxide, and hydrogen fluoride. Sulfur dioxide can cause acid rain and air pollution. Carbon dioxide is heavier than air, so it collects in low-lying areas. If too much collects in one place it can kill people and animals. Hydrogen fluoride in the ash coats plants and poisons the animals that eat them.

Landslides pose another danger. They can range from less than three feet (0.9 m) across to more than 100 feet (30 m) across. Rock and other debris move down the side of the volcano with so much force that the landslide can cross a valley and run up the side of another mountain. Landslides usually destroy everything in their paths.

If rain or other water is mixed in with the landslide, it is likely a lahar will develop. A mixture of water, rocks, and debris, lahars look a lot like masses of wet concrete rushing down the side of a volcano. Lahars vary in size

Mudflows known as lahars are among the deadliest effects of volcanoes.

Mount Saint Helens released an incredible amount of material from beneath the crust.

and shape, carrying everything from muddy clay to huge boulders. They can crush buildings, roads, and bridges. Anything left standing might be buried by the rock and debris left behind. Lahars put people in great danger. They usually move too fast for people to outrun.

The most deadly of the volcanic hazards is the pyroclastic flow. Hot gas and rock blast down the side of the volcano at speeds often greater than 50 miles per hour (80 kmh). Temperatures in the flow can reach more than 1,000 degrees Fahrenheit (540°C). Pyroclastic flows bury, shatter, and burn almost everything in their way.

MOUNT SAINT HELENS

In March 1980, earthquakes shook the ground near Mount Saint Helens in Washington State. One week later, steam and ash began to erupt from a small vent near the top. Although many people were surprised, scientists were not. In 1978, **geologists** noted how frequently the volcano erupted and predicted another violent eruption before the end of the century. They expected it would probably include lahars, lava flows, ashfall, landslides, and explosive gases.

They were right. Two years later, on the morning of May 18, 1980, an earthquake caused 1,300 feet (400 m) of mountaintop to crumble in the largest landslide in recorded history. A **lateral blast** of magma blew violently from the mountainside. A 650-mile-per-hour (1,050 kmh) wind carried rock, ash, and gas. It destroyed nearly everything over 230 square miles (600 sq km). The eruption continued for the next nine hours as landslides, lahars, and pyroclastic flows killed 57 people and countless plants and animals.

CHAPTER 5

SCIENCE SAVES LIVES

There is still a lot to learn about volcanoes. Many types of scientists are working hard to find out more about how to predict eruptions. Physical volcanologists study the ways volcanoes erupt by collecting and analyzing samples of toxic gases and lava. Geochemists study the rocks, gas, and lava that result from eruptions. Geophysicists study earthquakes to help monitor volcanic activity.

Using sophisticated tools, these scientists try to predict future eruptions. They know an increase in earthquakes often precedes an eruption. They use devices called tiltmeters to detect even the slightest change in the shape of a volcano. A bulge in a volcano can mean magma is rising.

Some scientists specialize in using satellites and cameras to sense volcanic hazards from far away. Thermal imaging cameras carried by airplanes or satellites take pictures of the heat coming from volcanoes. Then they can determine the age of lava flows. Radar mappers create three-dimensional maps of Earth's surface. These help scientists predict which direction lava flows or landslides might go.

VOLCANIC EXPLOSIVITY INDEX

Since the 1980s, scientists have used the Volcanic Explosivity Index (VEI) to describe the size of explosive volcanic eruptions on a scale of 0 to 8. To determine a number, scientists consider factors such as ashfall, pyroclastic flows, height of the eruption column, and how many hours the eruption lasts. Mount Saint Helens and Vesuvius were both given a VEI of 5.

Tourists can visit many slow-moving lava flows.

Volcanic eruptions can be devastating. But volcanoes and their eruptions are also beneficial. Volcanic deposits eventually break down and become some of the most fertile soil on Earth. Volcanoes rising from the ocean become islands, and lava flows create new land. Hot springs, health spas, and mud baths draw visitors to volcanic sites.

Volcanoes are fierce, powerful, terrifying forces of nature that can destroy life and land. And though there is still much to learn, scientists have proved that studying

How Science Works
KNOWING SIGNS, SAVING LIVES

If a volcano is changing in shape, it could be a sign that magma and gas are rising. Earthquakes near the site of a volcano indicate that movement is occurring underground. Volcanic gas rising from the vent can also mean an eruption will soon occur. These signs are common to many kinds of volcanoes. No matter where the volcano is on Earth, scientists use similar evidence to predict upcoming eruptions.

In 1991, scientists were able to use this type of information to predict the eruption of Mount Pinatubo in the Philippines. Scientists recognized key signs before Pinatubo erupted, giving thousands of people time to evacuate. Because of their work, at least 5,000 lives and $250 million in property were saved.

volcanoes is the first step in predicting where, when, and how they will erupt. As they improve their predictions, volcanologists will be able to save more lives.

TOP FIVE WORST
VOLCANIC ERUPTIONS

1. **Tambora, Indonesia, 1815**
   In the largest eruption ever recorded, Tambora killed at least 10,000 people with lava flows and toxic gases. At least 80,000 more died from starvation as the volcanic ash blocked out sunlight for months, causing crops to fail.

2. **Krakatoa, Indonesia, 1883**
   Krakatoa's enormous eruption caused entire villages to disappear. About 36,000 people lost their lives due to ash and toxic fumes.

3. **Mount Pelée, Martinique, 1902**
   Residents of Saint-Pierre on the island of Martinique in the Caribbean Sea had been watching the volcano for several days when it exploded. About 28,000 people died.

4. **Mount Ruiz, Colombia, 1985**
   Mount Ruiz killed about 23,000 people in the village of Armero. The eruption occurred at night when many were asleep.

5. **Vesuvius, Italy, 79**
   The people of Pompeii were killed and remained buried for centuries under ash and rock. An estimated 16,000 people died. In 1631, Vesuvius erupted again, this time killing approximately 4,000 people.

LEARN MORE

FURTHER READING

Furgang, Kathy. *Everything Volcanoes and Earthquakes*. Washington, DC: National Geographic, 2013.

Rusch, Elizabeth. *Eruption! Volcanoes and the Science of Saving Lives*. Boston, MA: Houghton Mifflin Harcourt, 2013.

Van Rose, Susanna. *Volcanoes and Earthquakes*. New York: DK, 2008.

WEB SITES

Discovery Kids—Volcano Explorer
http://kids.discovery.com/games/build-play/volcano-explorer
On this Web site, users can build their own volcanoes and see what happens when they erupt.

National Geographic—Volcanoes 101
http://video.nationalgeographic.com/video/kids/forces-of-nature-kids/volcanoes-101-kids
This Web site features a video to introduce readers to volcanoes.

GLOSSARY

crust (KRUST) the outer layer of Earth

geologists (jee-AWL-uh-jists) scientists who study Earth

lahars (luh-HAWRZ) mixes of water and rock traveling down the side of a volcano that look like wet concrete when flowing

lateral blast (lat-uh-ruhl BLAST) an eruption from the side of a volcano

magma (MAG-muh) hot, melted rock

magma chamber (MAG-muh chaym-buhr) an area of liquid rock underground

mantle (MAN-tuhl) the layer of Earth between the crust and the core

pyroclastic flow (pye-roh-klas-tic FLO) a fluid mixture of hot, dry rock fragments and toxic gases traveling at great speeds

rift (RIFT) an opening made by splitting or separation

subduction zones (sub-DUCKT-shun zohnz) places where tectonic plates move underneath each other

summit crater (SUM-it cray-tur) the top of a volcano

volcanologists (vawl-kuhn-AWL-uh-jists) scientists who study volcanoes

INDEX

[21ST CENTURY SKILLS LIBRARY]